About the Author

JM Young is a double-chartered professional technical consultant in the UK construction industry. As well as continually writing poetry, he works on novels and uses poetry to form ideas for stories. He is a proud Yorkshireman and has been happily married to his wife, Sue, for over thirty years. They live in South Yorkshire. He is a keen nature lover and enjoys long walks exploring his home county and the Peak District.

Human

James Young

Human

Olympia Publishers
London

www.olympiapublishers.com
OLYMPIA PAPERBACK EDITION

Copyright © James Young 2023

A CIP catalogue record for this title is
available from the British Library.

ISBN: 978-1-80439-086-3

First Published in 2023

Olympia Publishers
Tallis House
2 Tallis Street
London
EC4Y 0AB

Printed in Great Britain

Dedication

I dedicate this book to the love of my life, my wife, Sue. She is the kindest and most beautiful person I have ever known. I am a very lucky man to have found my soulmate.

Acknowledgements

Thank you to my wife, Sue, for all her support and encouragement in writing this book.

Special thanks to our friend Andrea for her invaluable contribution, advice and encouragement.

The Torment

You've seen beyond the dark.
You've lived behind the light.

To you, the truth is lies.
To you, life is a crime.

Your lies make you survive.
Your truth is where they hide.

Dark rages deep inside.
Light can't get through your eyes.

The secrets of the night.
Love burned out of sight.
The horrors of the mind.
The torment you must find.

What is it?

Child's Eyes

I once knew a boy who could imagine great things. He could run up a mountain, swim the depths of the sea. He could fly a jet fighter then come home for tea.

As life became real, his dreams were pushed further away. Responsibility overtakes dreams when there are bills you must pay.

I once knew a boy who could turn ice into flame. He could imagine a world totally free from all pain. He could visualize worlds by gazing at stars, see God up in heaven or meet him on Mars.

He knew that the boy would soon be a man. He accepted that Nature had its well-rehearsed plan.

I once knew a boy who could swim with sharks, live in outer space and drive the fastest of cars. He could run like the wind, see sunshine in the dark.

He could make enemies friends, feel the touch of the stars. He could fly like an eagle, create spaceships with sand, harness the power of the Universe in the palm of his hand.

I once knew a boy and still see him to this day; as I look in the mirror, he stares back in his way.

Though the imagination of childhood seems to have been buried away, I can see in his eyes it's still there and there to stay!

The Misty Mountain Whispers

The mist of the mountain stilled a stark silence and veiled
the presence of a haunting, menacing fate.
We heard the whispers of the white ghost and felt the
mountain quake.
The edges were sharp and fearsome, the going was causing
pain.
The snowy wind was freezing but we had to face the strain.
I turned to see you kneeling and fading in too much pain.
I wrapped my arms around you but knew it was in vain.
The mist of the mountain sat-stilled in frozen awe.
Two people who were freezing vanished forever more.
Claimed by the call of the white ghost. A dark spirit of the
mountain core.
The mist of the mountain whispers our doom to the fore.

Dancing Shadows

I stole a beat from the rain.
I stole a tune from the river.
In the black mirror, I'd look into the pain.
Something lost from this picture.
I heard the wind shout at the trees.
I saw the dancing of so many leaves.
I felt a tingling right there in the air.
I turned to see you not there.
I faced the cold and the dark.
I heard sirens screaming from afar.
I stood in the moonlight of night.
I reasoned on how I could fight.
But as the rain drummed the water and the ground
I heard a call from the crowd.
I saw a shadow of me in dark space.
I see a shimmer of love appear next to me.
A ghost in the black I can see.
Together again we can be.
Dancing shadows in the river.

War; What Is It Good For?

Remember that they had the chance to talk but they chose
not to speak.
They had the chance to listen but they chose not to hear.

Now young men are standing over there facing young men
over here.
Men who love their families, men who love their mums.
Soon they'll be cut to pieces under smoking machine guns.

But remember that they chose not to speak and remember
that they chose not to hear. Now all the men that they sent
to these lands will day by day disappear.

They could have chosen to talk and they could have chosen
to listen.

To DIE For

It felt so good like we were movie stars.
You were with me, my friends, in my souped-up car.
Through the village street at such high-octane speed.
Tyres screech, car screams, girls see.
Bump the kerb, skid through the bend. We are men in a car,
driving like this mission won't end.
Police give chase, blue lights flashing behind.
This is where the night changes from fun to wild.
Now forcing harder and sharper at corners and bends.
One mistake now and it all ends…
People gather near the pub.
Streetlights shine over all the blood.
Car is dead, crashed into a wall. Friends are dead, seat belts
an'all.
Policeman is the last one I see. Pain, blood, metal sticking
out of me.
He winces when he sees the bloody mess, looks into my eyes
with a sad grimace.
I hear the siren of the ambulance come. I turn my head to
see the paramedics run. I turn back to see the policeman in
the cold dark rain.
With tears in his eyes, he asks me my name.
I smile and before I can speak it to him… the sounds all
around me and my sight goes really dim.
Then blackness as I hear my father cry and my mother

scream.

My brothers are so sad, my kitten yowls on my bed in the night. He can't sleep.

A photo of me when I was in the scouts. A young smiling face with such promise and dreams, over a coffin with me in. My father still cries, my mother still screams.

Moonlight Passion

The music of the night played on-a distant beat out of sight.
Sounds echo in the air of broken dreams everywhere.
The stolen kisses in the dark, the secret whispers igniting sparks.
Lipstick marking on the skin show exactly where they've been.
Wild hair, wild passion found sensual dancing off the ground.
Neon lights on cold stone, slithering bodies entwined, moan.
Cold air soothes warm skin, dark shadows smother youth's grin.
Bright moon casts stark light on the fevers of passion in the night.
Burning desire spent now, eased tensions damped down.
Two people create a magic of their own.
Nameless faces remain unknown.
Feel the cold air of dawn setting in as the mind continues reliving.
Soft skin, warm lips, cold air and fingertips.
Tingling heat, beating heart, ruffled hair, ruffled clothes.
Streetlight finds a way home.
Wake to listen to your heartbeat, reliving the beautiful memory of a passionate moonlit dream.

Skin Tone Shades

To strive for decency is a better hope.
To strive for tolerance is a better dream.

To strive for kindness is a better human.
To strive for fairness is a better humanity.

To look and to listen and not hasten to act.
To feel and collaborate and not react.

To see each other through respectful eyes.
To accept each other without the lies.

To open our minds and see past the skin tone shades…
The world would be a much better place.

Holes

You may think he's weird. You may think she's odd.

Look deeper than the skin and see something you don't know, something you never thought of.

People are all different, finding different ways to heal.

People are all different, with unique ways to feel.

You may have a full heart ready and able to give love.

You may have a generous mind, always seeking to feel love.

But some minds and hearts don't have the range of what you can receive or give.

Exposed and beaten by life, a life you would not want to live.

Some hearts and minds have holes inside where nothing can get through.

Some hearts and minds are broken and there's little you can say or do.

Listen to their pain and sorrow and listen to them too.

Don't judge a broken heart or mind; because that's the worst thing you can do.

You Feed Yourself the Whys

You're fooling yourself.
You don't need that to fly.
You don't need that to burn.
You don't need that to cry.
Use it as an excuse.
Blot out reason for why.
Try to justify.
But don't expect me to see why.
You don't even try.
A day would soon go by.
A start of being dry.
But what the hell's the use
Trying to convince you
You don't need that to fly.
Let it rule your life.
Let it take control of your mind.
Why should you put up a fight?
Sit there, drink it all tonight.
Your pride's too proud to make the call.
To stand and look into your eyes.
To face up to your lies.
You feed yourself the whys.
The reasons you despise the man behind your eyes…
You don't listen to his cries.

Break the Odds

Deadbeat lost soul, no hope.
Nice guy, loyalty, good bloke.
Love found is no joke.
Ends meet but always broke.
Chance given, can he cope?

Outsider's chance of glory.
Just go the distance.
That's the best story.
Fight with the champ.

Toe to toe.
Blow to blow.
Live the dream.

Italian Stallion.
Break odds.

Rocky.

The Warm Red Planet with a Cold Black Stare

The air is cold out there.
There's something else out there.
There's something in the wind.
It's time to make us rescind.
We've lost this place, we've gone too far.
Life here may well one day flourish but now it won't hold
our hearts.
Our time is now and soon we will depart.
The ship is damaged beyond repair.
That sound you hear in the air?
To watch us perish without a care.
A laughing planet saying, 'Don't you dare.'
To bring our race here, our survival is not its care.
It knows that Earth has been stripped bare.
The warm, red planet with a cold, black stare.
It will rinse the stain of our attempt at life.
Freeze us off this bright red block of ice.

The Old Prides

The old rails for the old carts.
The soot stains on the old timbers.
The old smoke of the steam train.
In the cold air, a lost smell still lingers.
The old chugs of the old barge.
The towpaths with the hoof marks.
The stone bridge lit by the moon's arc.
The old man with his blackened pipe listens to the skylarks
as the daylight dwindles.
The old pride of a smart tie with a straight back and a warm
pint in the free time.
The old eyes over an old smile still twinkle.
The old prides of the old ways.
The past times of the old days.
The lost laughs from the old mates.
The shoeshine next to the fireplace.
The long line through your life's scape connects you back to
the old ways and a lost time where simple things did joy
make, in the world of your memories.

Broken

I did everything right but they took it away.
I did everything right, I worked hard every single day.
I did everything right, I didn't sleaze, crawl or whore.
I did everything right for you because it's you I adore.
I did everything right, I never hurt a living soul.
I did everything right and yet life demanded me go.
I did everything right because I chose not to do wrong.
I did everything right and still sang my own song.
But life narrows the road and it darkens the light.
It drains the marrow from your bones and makes you fight
for your life.
As I sit here alone on a bench and the cold freezes my pain
and troubles away,
I scrawl words that my body in death found will say...
I did everything right.

Those Days of Lawless Law

The eyes are the same.
We stared across the pub floor.
No other sign of recognition, just coldness in his glower.
So many years have gone by since the days of lawless law.

We saw the real thing.
We saw the real man.
The stench in the air, young death on the land.

I still hear you cry.
I still hear you beg for me to finish your life because of what
they'd done to your legs.
You once were my friend, my mate, my comrade.
I never saw you again after the hell of the trench.

Sixty years have gone by and there you are now, sitting not
ten yards away.
Trying to not recognize me?
Afraid to speak because of what you think I might say?

My brother, my brother, for what we saw; they'll never see!
For what we knew, they'll never know. For what we did,
they'll never do.
For what we understand, they'll never even consider.

It's me, it's me, please look at me, 'till my dying day you'll be
a brother to me.

Bitter Yorkshire Rain

The table feels like it did before.
Under my hands the wooden fibres go from cold to very warm.
The house feels colder tonight but now we are both here.
The same two people who invested everything they had right here.
Now I have listened to what you had to say.
I see our picture begin to fade.
I listen intently to the quiet night for some kind of winning message to come but then I realize I've lost this fight.
I understand now how this life works, I see the meaning and some of its quirks.
You say to me that I have to go on and live a life.
You say this to me and that I owe it to you, my wife.
But I sit here sometimes feeling nothing but the cold, dark pain.
I ask God and demand answers in the sharp and bitter Yorkshire rain.
But as usual nothing and no answers come and then you appear and talk to me like our life together has just begun.
But trapped I am in a mind of chaos, sorrow and despair.
For I see you here but I know...
that you're not there.

Blood, Love and Sorrow

I stare into your eyes. Your smile so full and bright.
I think of and hear the sound of your voice.
I close my eyes and see your soft skin touching me, I feel
your breath, your warmth, your grace, so near to me.

I hear the whistle go. I feel my heart becoming cold.
For now, the time is here. Time for innocence and love to
disappear.

I look at your smiling face. I say a prayer for you and the
human race.

I put your picture in my chest pocket next to my heart
hoping if I die, we will never part.

The sludge of mud and blood under feet. Running now
towards death soon to meet.
The thuds of men hitting the ground. The cries and screams
surround.

Fear takes a hold of me. Rage burns a hole in me.
I kill what's in front of me. Bayonet stabs so viciously.

I feel the temper die. I pretend I hear a lie. To retreat, to
retreat.

I see them come at me. Through the smoke, I hear their battle roars.
I am spent, I can fight no more.
Shot several times, I feel no pain. I hit the ground where I will remain.

I try to find the picture of you. I look at your pretty, smiling face.
My eyes subdue, I feel Death's embrace.
I tighten my grip around the picture of you as I rest my eyes to die knowing...
...I truly love you.

Without Gorm

Frank said, "What's the story?"
Sid said, "What story's that then?"
Frank looked at Sid, Sid looked at Frank.
Silence for a minute.
Gormless, both men.

"Slug ate my lettuce," Sid pointed to a corner near his shed.
"Eeeeeh, well tha' knows what that means don't ya?"
"What's that then?"
"Time for a cuppa tea Sid."
"Best put kettle on then."

"Strange things them slugs aren't they?"
"Pity, poor little buggers lost their shells, eh?"
"Shells, that's snails."
"Nails?"

Sid looked at Frank, Frank looked at Sid.
Silence for a minute.
Gormless, both men.

Made like My Grandad Used to Do

Ten stops down the line.
That's where the place is, the place I call mine.
Ten stops to go 'till I get home and let today go.
An old lady sits opposite me, smiles and says she's looking
forward to a hot cup of tea.
This pleasure of her day makes the cold go away. The
journey through the city and along the riverbank.
I ask if she has milk, sugar and biscuits to dunk? She smiles
and says she's very particular with her brew.
One and half teaspoons and no more; or it's quite simply a
poor do! A teaspoon of milk; gold top full cream or another
pour it will be!
I smile back and ask her why so precise with her tea?
She looks straight at me. It's my link back to my past.
An old friend of youth I've never lost.
Made like my grandad used to do. Like buttered corners on
his bread too. Buttered all over the slice of bread. That's
what my grandad always said.
So my cup of tea is part of me. With it I find I can relax
quite deeply. But it has to be just right. Or I won't relax
tonight you see.
Five stops down and she gets to her feet.
This is my stop she says to me.
Goodnight she says as she smiles at me.
Goodnight I say back but before she turns from me I say,
   "Enjoy your cup of tea."

Falling Rocks

It's hard to see the good when you're bombarded with the bad.

It's hard to crack a smile when your soul and mind are very sad.

It's hard to hear angels whisper when the demons start to sing.

It's hard to find the light when the horizon is so dim.

It's hard to feel humanity when you hear the animals scream and cry.

It's hard to see the reasoning when you get beaten for asking why.

It's hard to feel empathy when they burn your love away.

It's hard to keep your temper when fools provoke you in every way.

It's hard to walk a straight line when life keeps twisting all your dreams.

It's hard to trust another when no one is who they seem.

It's hard to find comfort when the rocks begin to fall.

It's hard to feel compassion when you're beating down every wall.

It's hard to find the sanity lurking in the back of your mind.

It's hard to listen to nothing when inside, you start to cry.

It's hard to see the point of it when you know how easy it is to take away.

It's hard to keep your grip on life when it changes every second of every minute of every day.

Give One Hundred Per cent

One hundred per cent, can you see it?
Maybe – imagine if that were a pool.
A pool of water, maybe or a pool of blood?

What power dictates true endeavour?
What justifies what stakes rise?
Perhaps we stand here in front of pure evil?
Perhaps it's pure love we see under a reddening sky?

How dangerous is it?
How sharp is the hand that slices to kill?
How blunt is the fist that strikes for the freedoms of you
and me to survive?

One hundred per cent is every fibre, every thought, every
sight seen through the eyes and deep in the mind's eye. All
the pumping blood, heartbeats, memories of love and hate
draining into the sea, rotting on the ground or exploding in
the vast sky.
Every feeling felt, every tear, scream or cry in an instant goes
by.

What of those who give one hundred per cent for our lands,
for our democracy?
What of those out there today or tonight?

To give one hundred per cent for most is too much because you can never be free.

To give one hundred per cent for those whom they love, do they separate themselves from humanity?

Imagine the pool of darkening water, imagine the lonely cloud in the deep blue sky.

One hundred per cent is everything; a whole life of hopes and dreams.

Don't you see?

Those who truly give one hundred per cent on the battlefields, in foreign seas or skies fighting for our liberty…

…die.

Behind the Skin

Why do you laugh at me when you know my pain?
Why do you insult me when you see my name?

Am I so different to be subjected to all this hate?
Am I so different that I can't be your mate?

Where does the border cross in the mind of you?
An invisible line on the ground that caused the deaths of
many people like me and you.

So I stand and I ask of you – do you just hate the colour of
my skin, or do you hate the human behind it too?

No One and No One

Look at me, for I am here.
The lonely life that they abused and tried to disappear.
The broken person with his broken mind.
I live amongst you all, but you are all blind.

Touch my hand and feel my skin.
I feel like you feel, but for me, no one feels from within.
I am skin and bone in physical space.
Yet my presence is lost in view like I have no face.

I walk the streets alone, no one bothers with me.
I see you enjoying living a life with a family.
You catch a glimpse of me in a dark silhouette.
Just for a second, I exist, but then you forget.

I can't live like you, I can't love like you.
For love forsook my life the day I was born.
They broke my bones; I never had a home.

They left me to feed on scraps and filth.
They beat me when I cried or asked for help.

Please look at me, for I am here.
The scars on my body will never disappear.

The war in my mind of life and death.
The whispered words I only talk to myself are just wasted breath.

Look at me for here I am on my knees, begging for anything.

Why walk past me?
Why help me feed?

For to you who has everything, I am no one and no one is me.

Evil Found

The dying leaves and decaying bark.
The ether of silent sorrow stark.
The earth feels like a distant moon.
The sun, a glowing bloom, totally helpless to their doom.

Nothing here can be real.
Nothing here can we feel.
No sound but the whimpering of lost souls.
They can't even cry – they're just bags of bones.

Swallow deep, swallow hard.
Straighten your back, stand hard.
Fight back tears, fists lock behind your back.
Clenched jaw ringing in your ears.
This sight will never leave your fears.

How can man be brought to this?
How can man do this, yet love and kiss?
What other animal on the earth is so destructive to its fellow
birth?
What other animal is so cruel?
We stand and look on like pathetic fools.

The gates are forced, these people can't run.
They stand around, they can't speak, but they're not dumb.

Stacked in piles, all dignity erased. Burning flesh, a damn awful smell of senseless, barbaric waste.

Hardened, liberating soldiers fall to their knees, crying, afraid of what they can see.
They trained for war, they didn't train for this.
They were prepared to die, they weren't prepared for this.

This stain of shame will always remain human, for this cannot be forgiven, for this cannot be forgotten.
It's hard to comprehend.
It's hard to understand.
How men can create hell on earth
How men can create concentration camps!

You Were in My Dream

You were in my dream.
What does it mean?
You were by my side when we had to hide.

We saw the shooting stars.
We saw the moonlit glistening lake.
We heard the wind in the trees.
We felt the cold embrace.

You were in my dream.
You were there with me.
You've seen what I've seen.
You were in my dream.
What does it mean?

I see you standing there.
Standing without a care.
Then you turn your head and see me.
You turn upon your feet.
You walk straight up to me.
You stand in front of me.

We're strangers, but together we have been
We're strangers, but together we've seen
We're strangers, never before did we meet

You look at me so quizzically, nodding then shaking your head, you say to me...
"How can this be? You were in my dream."

Portrait of a Lady

Tree branches spread over the sky.
Birds flitting about here and there.
The sun beaming low in the sky.
The sounds of Spring in the air.

We walked through the woods without a care.
A face beckoned a smile.
We felt quite at ease.
A woman with a heart-warming smile and such beautiful
caring eyes.
Her long dark hair feeling the breeze.

We walked past where she had sat down.
She commented on the sun's rays lighting the house.
We nodded in appreciation as we looked and agreed.
Surrounded by rolling hills of green, it looked like the Jewel
of the Crown.
She wished us well on our way.

We carried on our walk to the house.
As we walked through the rooms, an old lady guide saw as
we stared from a window over the grounds.
She said "that's where the lady would sit watching the sun's
rays lighting the woods and the hills.
She died of a broken heart when her love had died fighting

in the Somme battlefields".

We could see why she would find some peace and happiness, such beauty, such magnificence without comparison.
As we walked in the next room, she presented a portrait of a lady on a seat looking down at the house with pale skin and dark hair.
We stood amazed, totally confounded! The lady in the portrait was the lady we had just met outside!

Scene So Clean

Is your faith your remedy?
Do you see past what others see?
No. But you stand and talk to me.
Not about what this is or what it means to me.
You talk to me, not with me, you talk at me!

What some prophet did or didn't do.
What the hell does that mean to this lowly little fool?
That is your cross, you don't put that weight on me.
When life is so cruel, so God damn constantly.
It doesn't matter, it just does not matter.

To believe like you believe.
Man, I wish I could see that scene so clean. Truth and lie,
black or white with no in-between.

What is it I see you ask of me?
All the distorted imagery, a life born out of fear, pain and
misery.
Humanity's reality is what you see in front of thee.
It doesn't matter.

Your faith is yours, you see.
Like your car or your house, it just does not mean the same
to me.

It doesn't matter.

You watch me bleed, but you don't 'feel' me.
I can't run so with your scripts of words you speak at me.
It doesn't matter.

Please let me sit here quietly in this pool of red you see of
me.
I came in here for peace, you see, to go out alone and
quietly.
I don't want your clemency; can your faith let you do that for
me?
Can you stand there silently? Let me be what I want to be.
Not one more day of this life for me.
'cos in a few more minutes, you'll see...

It doesn't matter.

The World Was Bigger than the Day and Night

Remember when you were a child?
The days of hope and the days of wild.

The furry trees and Christmas lights.
The smell of grass on long summer nights.

Remember looking into the sky?
The world was bigger than the day and night.

You chased your dreams down streets and through the fields.
You sang the innocence that only childhood sings.

Remember when you could play and run all through the
night?
The winds and rain could not ease your might.

The night seemed forever and forever was so very far.
You could see the light of every star.

Remember that little young version of you?
The fears and tears of what growing up would do.
The pain and laughter that you'd never thought you'd own.

Remember when you first fell in love?

The world was magic and full of good.
That other person who wanted you.

Remember those days because they're what made you you.

If It's Real, It Ain't Fake

Shallow.
Your words fall not too far.
Shallow.
Your morals are what you are.

Love.
Love can carry any of your promises' weight.
Love.
If it's real, it ain't fake.

Living.
Did you sell yourself a lie?
Living.
Anything to get by?

You.
You're living a shallow lie.
You.
You love living only the good times.
Pretending youth is still on your side.

Us.
Deeper feelings come with age.
Us.
Togetherness is a road of two ways.

You expect the depths of the Pacific from my side, but you don't even have a tide.

They Want Me to Speak Now You're Gone

They want me to speak now you're gone.
Find some kind of peace or something to hold on.
They want me to talk about you, the love you gave… but I
just cannot do.

You only gave me fear.
You only gave me tears.
If love for you is me a slave, love must be what you made.
I'm broken and hollow without you but at least now you're
gone, fear isn't living here too.

I can't say the words they want me to say.
I can't feel love when for years, you treated me 'your' way.
The drinking that led to the bruises and blood.
The silence of being locked alone in a dark room.
The insults you were happy to give.
The pain you dispensed so lucidly.

Now that you've died and gone away.
I find myself looking at you this day.
I hope that where you are now.
You realize what you did in breaking me down.

I can't sleep without help.
I can't weep for you or myself.

I can't sing or dance any more.
You took so much for yourself and broke something that I
can't restore.